The Fifteen M of Saint B

MW00897276

Revealed by Our Lord to Saint Bridget of Sweden

Table of Contents

The Fifteen Magnificent Prayers of Saint Bridget of Sweden.................1
Revealed by Our Lord to Saint Bridget of Sweden.....................1
Introduction...5
First Prayer..6
Second Prayer...8
Third Prayer..9
Fourth Prayer...10
Fifth Prayer..11
Sixth Prayer...12
Seventh Prayer..13
Eighth Prayer...14
Ninth Prayer..15
Tenth Prayer..16
Eleventh Prayer..17
Twelfth Prayer..18
Thirteenth Prayer...19
Fourteenth Prayer...20
Fifteenth Prayer..21
Conclusion...22
Warning..23

Introduction

This devotion was given by Jesus to Saint Bridget so that by saying these fifteen Prayers with an Our Father and Hail Mary before each, we might honor each wound Jesus received in His scourging.

First Prayer

Our Father, Hail Mary

O Jesus Christ! Eternal Sweetness to those who love Thee, joy surpassing all joy and all desire, Salvation and Hope of all sinners, Who hast proved that thou hast no greater desire than to be among men, even assuming human nature at the fullness of time for the love of men, recall all the sufferings Thou hast endured from the instant of Thy conception, and especially during Thy Passion, as it was decreed and ordained from all eternity in the Divine plan.

Remember, O Lord, that during the Last Supper with Thy disciples, having washed their feet, Thou gavest them Thy Most Precious Body and Blood, and while at the same time Thou didst sweetly console them, Thou didst foretell them thy coming Passion.

Remember the sadness and bitterness which Thou didst experience in Thy Soul as Thou Thyself bore witness saying: "My Soul is sorrowful even unto death."

Remember all the fear, anguish and pain that Thou didst suffer in Thy delicate Body before the torment of the Crucifixion, when, after having prayed three times, bathed in a sweat of blood, Thou wast betrayed by Judas, Thy disciple, arrested by the people of a nation Thou hadst chosen and elevated, accused by false witnesses, unjustly judged by three judges during the flower of Thy youth and during the solemn Paschal season.

Remember that Thou wast despoiled of Thy garments and clothed in those of derision; that Thy Face and

Eyes were veiled, that Thou wast buffeted, crowned with thorns, a reed placed in Thy Hands, that Thou was crushed with blows and overwhelmed with affronts and outrages.

In memory of all these pains and sufferings which Thou didst endure before Thy Passion on the Cross, grant me before my death true contrition, a sincere and entire confession, worthy satisfaction and the remission of all my sins. Amen.

Second Prayer

Our Father, Hail Mary

O Jesus! True liberty of angels, Paradise of delights, remember the horror and sadness which Thou didst endure when Thy enemies, like furious lions, surrounded Thee, and by thousands of insults, spits, blows, lacerations and other unheard of cruelties, tormented Thee at will. In consideration of these torments and insulting words, I beseech Thee, O my Savior, to deliver me from all my enemies, visible and invisible, and to bring me, under Thy protection, to the perfection of eternal salvation. Amen.

Third Prayer

Our Father, Hail Mary

O Jesus! Creator of Heaven and earth Whom nothing can encompass or limit, Thou Who dost enfold and hold all under Thy Loving power, remember the very bitter pain Thou didst suffer when the Jews nailed Thy Sacred Hands and Feet to the Cross by blow after blow with big blunt nails, and not finding Thee in a pitiable enough state to satisfy their rage, they enlarged Thy Wounds, and added pain to pain, and with indescribable cruelty stretched Thy Body on the Cross, pulled Thee from all sides, thus dislocating Thy Limbs. I beg of Thee, O Jesus, by the memory of this most Loving suffering of the Cross, to grant me the grace to fear Thee and to Love Thee. Amen.

Fourth Prayer

Our Father, Hail Mary

O Jesus! Heavenly Physician, raised aloft on the Cross to heal our wounds with Thine, remember the bruises which Thou didst suffer and the weakness of all Thy Members which were distended to such a degree that never was there pain like unto Thine. From the Crown of Thy Head to the Soles of Thy Feet there was not one spot on Thy Body that was not in torment, and yet, forgetting all Thy sufferings, Thou didst not cease to pray to Thy Heavenly Father for Thy enemies, saying: "Father forgive them for they know not what they do."

Through this great Mercy, and in memory of this suffering, grant that the remembrance of Thy Most Bitter Passion may effect in us a perfect contrition and the remission of all our sins. Amen.

Fifth Prayer

Our Father, Hail Mary

O Jesus! Mirror of eternal splendor, remember the sadness which Thou experienced, when contemplating in the light of Thy Divinity the predestination of those who would be saved by the merits of Thy Sacred Passion, Thou didst see at the same time, the great multitude of reprobates who would be damned for their sins, and Thou didst complain bitterly of those hopeless lost and unfortunate sinners.

Through this abyss of compassion and pity, and especially through the goodness which Thou displayed to the good thief when Thou saidst to him: "This day, thou shalt be with Me in Paradise." I beg of Thee, O Sweet Jesus, that at the hour of my death, Thou wilt show me mercy. Amen.

Sixth Prayer

Our Father, Hail Mary

O Jesus! Beloved and most desirable King, remember the grief Thou didst suffer, when naked and like a common criminal, Thou was fastened and raised on the Cross, when all Thy relatives and friends abandoned Thee, except Thy Beloved Mother, who remained close to Thee during Thy agony and whom Thou didst entrust to Thy faithful disciple when Thou saidst to Mary: "Woman, behold thy son!" and to Saint John: "Son, behold thy Mother!" I beg of Thee, O my Savior, by the sword of sorrow which pierced the soul of Thy Holy Mother, to have compassion on me in all my afflictions and tribulations, both corporal and spiritual, and to assist me in all my trials, and especially at the hour of my death. Amen.

Seventh Prayer

Our Father, Hail Mary

O Jesus! Inexhaustible Fountain of compassion, Who by a profound gesture of Love, said from the Cross: "I thirst!" suffered from the thirst for the salvation of the human race. I beg of Thee, O my Savior, to inflame in our hearts the desire to tend toward perfection in all our acts; and to extinguish in us the concupiscence of the flesh and the ardor of worldly desires. Amen.

Eighth Prayer

Our Father, Hail Mary

O Jesus! Sweetness of hearts, delight of the spirit, by the bitterness of the vinegar and gall which Thou didst taste on the Cross for Love of us, grant us the grace to receive worthily Thy Precious Body and Blood during our life and at the hour of our death, that they may serve as a remedy and consolation for our souls. Amen.

Ninth Prayer

Our Father, Hail Mary

O Jesus! Royal virtue, joy of the mind, recall the pain Thou didst endure, when, plunged in an ocean of bitterness at the approach of death, insulted, outraged by the Jews, Thou didst cry out in a loud voice that Thou was abandoned by Thy Father, saying: "My God, My God, why hast Thou forsaken me?" Through this anguish, I beg of Thee, O my Savior, not to abandon me in the terrors and pains of my death. Amen.

Tenth Prayer

Our Father, Hail Mary

O Jesus! Who art the beginning and end of all things, life and virtue, remember that for our sakes, Thou was plunged in an abyss of suffering from the soles of Thy Feet to the crown of Thy Head. In consideration of the enormity of Thy Wounds, teach me to keep, through pure love, Thy Commandments, whose way is wide and easy for those who love Thee. Amen.

Eleventh Prayer

Our Father, Hail Mary

O Jesus! Deep abyss of mercy, I beg of Thee, in memory of Thy Wounds, which penetrated to the very marrow of Thy Bones and to the depth of Thy Being, to draw me, a miserable sinner, overwhelmed by my offenses, away from sin and to hide me from Thy Face justly irritated against me, hide me in Thy Wounds, until Thy anger, and just indignation, shall have passed away. Amen.

Twelfth Prayer

Our Father, Hail Mary

O Jesus! Mirror of Truth, symbol of unity, link of Charity, remember the multitude of wounds with which Thou was covered from Head to Foot, torn and reddened by the spilling of Thy Adorable Blood.

O Great and Universal Pain which Thou didst suffer in Thy Virginal Flesh for Love of us! Sweetest Jesus!

What is there, that Thou couldst have done for us, which Thou hast not done! May the fruit of Thy sufferings, be renewed in my soul by the faithful remembrance of Thy Passion, and may Thy Love increase in my heart each day, until I see Thee in eternity, Thou Who art the treasury of every real good and every joy, which I beg Thee to grant me, O Sweetest Jesus, in Heaven. Amen.

Thirteenth Prayer

Our Father, Hail Mary

O Jesus! Strong Lion, Immortal and Invincible King, remember the pain which Thou didst endure, when all Thy strength, both moral and physical, was entirely exhausted, Thou didst bow Thy Head, saying: "It is consummated!" Through this anguish and grief, I beg of Thee Lord Jesus, to have mercy on me at the hour of my death, when my mind will be greatly troubled and my soul will be in anguish. Amen.

Fourteenth Prayer

Our Father, Hail Mary

O Jesus! Only Son of the Father, Splendor and Figure of His Substance, remember the simple and humble recommendation, Thou didst make of Thy Soul to Thy Eternal Father, saying: "Father, into Thy Hands I commend My Spirit!" And with Thy Body all torn, and Thy Heart Broken, and the bowels of Thy Mercy open to redeem us, Thou didst Expire. By this Precious Death, I beg of Thee O King of Saints, comfort me and help me to resist the devil, the flesh and the world, so that being dead to the world I may live for Thee alone.

I beg of Thee at the hour of my death to receive me, a pilgrim and an exile returning to Thee. Amen.

Fifteenth Prayer

Our Father, Hail Mary

O Jesus! True and Fruitful Vine! Remember the abundant outpouring of Blood, which, Thou didst so generously shed from Thy Sacred Body, as juice from grapes in a wine press.

From Thy Side, pierced, with a lance by a soldier, blood and water issued forth, until, there was not left in Thy Body a single drop, and finally, like a bundle of myrrh lifted to the top of the Cross, Thy delicate Flesh was destroyed, the very Substance of Thy Body withered, and the Marrow of Thy Bones dried up.

Through this bitter Passion and through the outpouring of Thy Precious Blood, I beg of Thee, O Sweet Jesus, to receive my soul when I am in my death agony. Amen.

Conclusion

O Sweet Jesus! Pierce my heart, so that my tears of penitence and love, will be my bread, day and night; may I be converted entirely to Thee, and may my heart be Thy perpetual habitation, may my conversation be pleasing to Thee, and may the end of my life, be so praiseworthy, that I may merit Heaven, and there with Thy saints, I may praise Thee forever. Amen.

Warning

A Monitum [warning] of the Holy Office: In certain places a booklet with the title: <u>The Secret of Happiness: Fifteen Prayers Revealed by Our Lord to Saint Brigid in the Church of Saint Paul in Rome</u>, published in various languages at Nice (and elsewhere).

Since it is asserted in this booklet that certain promises were made by God to Saint Brigid, and it is by no means certain that these promises were of supernatural origin, Ordinaries of places must avoid giving permission to publish or reprint works or writings which contain the aforesaid promises.

Given at Rome, from the Holy Office, 28 January, 1954.[1]

Note well the prayers are approved by the Church, but the promises that were circulating have been forbidden to be published. We remind people of this, because these promises are in circulation to this day. We wish always to be in full conformity with the holy Catholic Church.

---

[1] Canon Law Digest, Volume 4, Page 389 AAS 46-64 Monitum 28 January, 1954 Promises of Saint Brigid not to be published.

Made in United States
Troutdale, OR
12/11/2024

26310994R00015